Let's Imagine

stories written by Farrah McDoogle
illustrated by Tom Brannon

Contents

studio **fun** BOOKS

White Plains, New York • Montréal, Québec • Bath, United Kingdom

Food, Yummy Food!

It was five minutes past lunchtime, and Cookie Monster's tummy was rumbling! "Me need nutrients, fast!" Cookie cried. In the kitchen he found apples and bananas, peas and corn, and one great, big roly-poly meatball.

"This food so yummy!" Cookie exclaimed between mouthfuls. "And healthy, too! How about that?"

Cookie's tummy stopped grumbling. "Me think me have room for one more food!" Cookie said, choosing a cookie—a great, big, crunchy cookie. "Since me eat so many healthy foods, it okay for me to have sometimes food like nice COOKIE!"

Finally, Cookie was full...until dinnertime!

Play Song 1

C Is for Cookie

Lyrics and music by Joe Raposo

C is for cookie, that's good enough for me.
C is for cookie, that's good enough for me.
C is for cookie, that's good enough for me.
Oh, cookie, cookie, cookie starts with C.

Oh, C is for cookie, that's good enough for me.
C is for cookie, that's good enough for me.
C is for cookie, that's good enough for me.
Oh, cookie, cookie, cookie starts with C.

So, C is for cookie, that's good enough for me.
C is for cookie, that's good enough for me.
C is for cookie, that's good enough for me.
Oh, cookie, cookie, cookie starts with C.
Yeah, cookie, cookie, cookie starts with C.
Oh, boy! Cookie, cookie, cookie starts with C.

Play
Song 2

Apples and Bananas

I like to eat, eat, eat apples and bananas.
I like to eat, eat, eat apples and bananas.

I like to ate, ate, ate ay-ples and bay-nay-nays.
I like to ate, ate, ate ay-ples and bay-nay-nays.

I like to eet, eet, eet ee-ples and bee-nee-nees.
I like to eet, eet, eet ee-ples and bee-nee-nees.

I like to ite, ite, ite i-ples and bi-ni-nis.
I like to ite, ite, ite i-ples and bi-ni-nis.

I like to ote, ote, ote o-ples and bo-no-nos.
I like to ote, ote, ote o-ples and bo-no-nos.

I like to oot, oot, oot oo-ples and boo-noo-noos.
I like to oot, oot, oot oo-ples and boo-noo-noos.

Play Song 3

Sing a Song of Sixpence

Sing a song of sixpence,
a pocket full of rye;
four and twenty blackbirds
baked in a pie!

When the pie was opened,
the birds began to sing.
Wasn't that a dainty dish
to set before a king?

Play
Song 4

The Muffin Man

Oh, do you know the muffin man,
the muffin man, the muffin man?
Oh, do you know the muffin man
that lives on Drury Lane?

Oh, yes, I know the muffin man,
the muffin man, the muffin man.
Oh, yes, I know the muffin man
that lives on Drury Lane.

Polly, Put the Kettle On

Polly, put the kettle on,
Polly, put the kettle on,
Polly, put the kettle on,
we'll all have tea.

Sukey, take it off again,
Sukey, take it off again,
Sukey, take it off again,
they've all gone away.

Blow the fire and make the toast.
Put the muffins on to roast.
Blow the fire and make the toast,
we'll all have tea.

Play
Song 6

Oats, Peas, Beans, & Barley Grow

Chorus:
Oats, peas, beans, and barley grow.
Oats, peas, beans, and barley grow.
Can you or I or anyone know
how oats, peas, beans, and barley grow?

Verse 1:
Thus the farmer sows the seed.
Thus he stands and takes his ease.
He stamps his foot and claps his hands,
and turns around and views the land. *(Chorus)*

Additional verses:
Next the farmer waters the seed, etc. (Chorus)
Next the farmer hoes the weeds, etc. (Chorus)
Last the farmer harvests the seed, etc. (Chorus)

It's Fun to Imagine

Whump, whump, whump! Elmo wonders if you have ever seen a helicopter in the sky. Whenever Elmo sees one, Elmo thinks about what Sesame Street would look like from there. How about we imagine that together?

Wow! Everything looks different from way up here! It's like the map on the wall at Elmo's school. Elmo sees trees and railroads. Look! Elmo can see the ocean. And there's Elmo's neighborhood! Do you see it? All the people look like itty-bitty dots, even big people, like firefighters. And the cars look like toy cars.

Pretending you're flying in a helicopter over your neighborhood is really fun, isn't it? But Elmo thinks it's more fun to be on the ground at home, because there's no better place to be!

People in Your Neighborhood

Lyrics and music by Jeff Moss

Oh, who are the people in your neighborhood,
in your neighborhood,
in your neighborhood?
Say, who are the people in your neighborhood,
the people that you meet each day?

Oh, the postman always brings the mail
through rain or snow or sleet or hail.
"I'll work and work the whole day through
to get your letter safe to you."

'Cause a postman is a person in your neighborhood,
in your neighborhood.
He's in your neighborhood.
A postman is a person in your neighborhood,
a person that you meet each day.

Oh, a fireman is brave, it's said.
His engine is a shiny red.
"If there's a fire anywhere about,
well, I'll be sure to put it out."

'Cause a fireman is a person in your neighborhood,
in your neighborhood.
He's in your neighborhood,
and a postman is a person in your neighborhood.
Well, they're the people that you meet
when you're walkin' down the street.
They're the people that you meet each day.

I've Been Working on the Railroad

I've been working on the railroad,
all the live-long day.
I've been working on the railroad,
just to pass the time away.
Don't you hear the whistle blowing?
Rise up so early in the morn.
Don't you hear the captain shouting,
"Dinah, blow your horn"?

Chorus (sing twice):
Dinah, won't you blow,
Dinah, won't you blow,
Dinah, won't you blow
your horn?

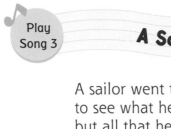
A Sailor Went to Sea

A sailor went to sea, sea, sea,
to see what he could see, see, see,
but all that he could see, see, see,
was the bottom of the deep blue sea, sea, sea.

Hey, Diddle Diddle

Hey, diddle diddle,
the cat and the fiddle,
the cow jumped over the moon.
The little dog laughed to see such sport
and the dish ran away with the spoon.

If All the Raindrops

If all the raindrops
were lemon drops and gumdrops,
oh, what a rain it would be!
I'd stand outside with my mouth open wide going,
"Ah, ah, ah-ah, ah, ah-ah, ah, ah-ah!"
If all the raindrops
were lemon drops and gumdrops,
oh, what a rain it would be!

Down by the Bay

Down by the bay
where the watermelons grow,
back to my home
I dare not go.
For if I do, my mother will say,
"Did you ever see a bear
combing his hair
down by the bay?"

Down by the bay
where the watermelons grow,
back to my home
I dare not go.
For if I do, my mother will say,
"Did you ever see a whale
with a polka-dot tail
down by the bay?"